J   Thomas, Rachael L.
613
.69   Make a light your way! :
THO   inventing gadgets to
        see in the dark

Super Simple DIY
SURVIVAL

MAKE A LIGHT YOUR WAY!

Inventing Gadgets to See in the Dark

RACHAEL L. THOMAS

CONSULTING EDITOR, DIANE CRAIG,
M.A./READING SPECIALIST

Super Sandcastle

An Imprint of Abdo Publishing
abdobooks.com

abdobooks.com

Printed in the United States of America, North Mankato, Minnesota
052019
092019

THIS BOOK CONTAINS
RECYCLED MATERIALS

Design: Tamara JM Peterson, Mighty Media, Inc.
Production: Mighty Media, Inc.
Editor: Megan Borgert-Spaniol
Cover Photographs: Mighty Media, Inc.; Shutterstock Images
Interior Photographs: Gibby Zobel; Mighty Media, Inc.; Shutterstock Images

The following manufacturers/names appearing in this book are trademarks:
ACDelco®, Duck Tape®, Elmer's®, littleBits™, Squishy Circuits™, Velcro®

Library of Congress Control Number: 2018967160

Publisher's Cataloging-in-Publication Data

Names: Thomas, Rachael L., author.
Title: Make a light your way!: inventing gadgets to see in the dark / by Rachael L. Thomas
Other title: Inventing gadgets to see in the dark
Description: Minneapolis, Minnesota : Abdo Publishing, 2020 | Series: Super simple diy survival
Identifiers: ISBN 9781532119750 (lib. bdg.) | ISBN 9781532174513 (ebook)
Subjects: LCSH: Outdoor recreation--Safety measures--Juvenile literature. | Survival skills--Juvenile literature. | Camping--Equipment and supplies--Juvenile literature. | Do-it-yourself work--Juvenile literature.
Classification: DDC 613.69--dc23

Super SandCastle™ books are created by a team of professional educators, reading specialists, and content developers around five essential components—phonemic awareness, phonics, vocabulary, text comprehension, and fluency—to assist young readers as they develop reading skills and strategies and increase their general knowledge. All books are written, reviewed, and leveled for guided reading and early reading intervention programs for use in shared, guided, and independent reading and writing activities to support a balanced approach to literacy instruction.

TO ADULT HELPERS

The projects in this book are fun and simple. There are just a few things to remember to keep kids safe. Some projects may use sharp or hot objects. Also, kids may be using messy supplies. Make sure they protect their clothes and work surfaces. Be ready to offer guidance during brainstorming and assist when necessary.

CONTENTS

BECOME A MAKER

A makerspace is like a laboratory. It's a place where ideas are formed and problems are solved. Kids like you create wonderful things in makerspaces. Many makerspaces are in schools and libraries. But they can also be in kitchens, bedrooms, and backyards. Anywhere can be a makerspace when you use imagination, inspiration, **collaboration**, and problem-solving!

IMAGINATION

This takes you to new places and lets you experience new things. Anything is possible with imagination!

INSPIRATION

This is the spark that gives you an idea. Inspiration can come from almost anywhere!

Makerspace Toolbox

COLLABORATION

Makers work together. They ask questions and get ideas from everyone around them. **Collaboration** solves problems that seem impossible.

PROBLEM-SOLVING

Things often don't go as planned when you're creating. But that's part of the fun! Find creative **solutions** to any problem that comes up. These will make your project even better.

SKILLS TO SURVIVE

Being a maker means being ready for anything. Your makerspace toolbox can even help you survive! People with survival skills learn to think fast and problem-solve. They find ways to stay safe and get help in **dangerous** situations.

You don't have to be in danger to use survival skills. These skills can come in handy if you're camping out in a tent. Or they might help you if your home's power goes out!

PROBLEM-SOLVE!
See page 26

BASIC NEEDS

Imagine you are lost in the woods or caught in a storm. What do you do? To survive, humans must make sure their basic needs are met. When you're building gear to help you survive, keep these basic needs in mind!

Air   First Aid   Water   Shelter and Warmth   Sleep   Food   Help!

IMAGINE A LIGHT

DISCOVER AND EXPLORE

Think about all the times you turn on a light. You probably use light to search your basement or see your dinner. Light helps you complete these tasks safely. But it could also help you follow trails or signal for rescue. And with a little creativity, light can do much more!

GET INSPIRED!
See page 24

IMAGINE

If you could **design** a light that could do anything, what would it do? Would it light the path in front of you? Would it flash to signal your location? Then, imagine a situation where you could use a light to survive. Are you exploring a dark cave? Are you lost in a shadowy forest? Remember, there are no rules. Let your imagination run wild!

EMERGENCY LIGHT

9

DESIGN A LIGHT

It's time to turn your dream light into a makerspace marvel! Think about your imaginary light and survival situation. How can the features of your light help you survive? How could you use the materials around you to create these features? Where would you begin?

Solar-powered lights take in the sun's energy during the day. This stored energy makes the lights shine at night. Solar-powered lights can be useful during outdoor adventures!

COLLABORATE!
See page 28

BE SAFE, BE RESPECTFUL
MAKERSPACE ETIQUETTE

THERE ARE JUST A FEW RULES TO FOLLOW WHEN YOU ARE BUILDING YOUR LIGHT:

1. **ASK FOR PERMISSION AND ASK FOR HELP.** Make sure an adult says it's OK to make your light. Get help when using sharp tools, such as a craft knife, or hot tools, like a glue gun.

2. **BE NICE.** Share supplies and space with other makers.

3. **THINK IT THROUGH.** Don't give up when things don't work out exactly right. Instead, think about the problem you are having. What are some ways to solve it?

4. **CLEAN UP.** Put materials away when you are finished working. Find a safe space to store unfinished projects until next time.

WHAT WILL YOUR LIGHT DO?

How will your light help you meet your basic needs? Knowing this will help you figure out which materials to use.

Will it signal for help? Then use tall, sturdy materials to build an eye-catching **beacon**.

A lighthouse is a beacon that helps guide ships at sea.

DIY!

PROBLEM-SOLVE!
See page 26

Will it hang in your tent?
Then use lightweight materials to create a hanging glow lamp!

IMAGINE

WHAT COULD YOU BUILD TO CONNECT YOUR LIGHT TO THE WALL OR CEILING?

In 2002, Brazilian inventor Alfredo Moser created a bottle light. He drilled a hole in his roof and stuck a water bottle in it. The water **refracted** outdoor sunlight. Using these water bottles, Moser filled his home with light!

LEDs are devices that give off light when electricity passes through them.

Will it light the path ahead? Then build a flashlight with an LED, wire, and **batteries**.

COLLABORATE!
See page 28

Will it be wearable?
Then try shaping **flexible** glow sticks to fit your body!

⚠ STUCK?

YOU CAN ALWAYS CHANGE YOUR MIND IN A MAKERSPACE. DO YOU WANT YOUR FLASHLIGHT TO BE HANDS-FREE? ATTACH IT TO A HELMET TO MAKE A HEADLAMP!

BUILD YOUR LIGHT

Lights come in many shapes and sizes. You can make a light using materials that glow in the dark. You could also make an electric light. If so, build your circuit and make sure it works. Then you can construct your **gadget** around the completed light.

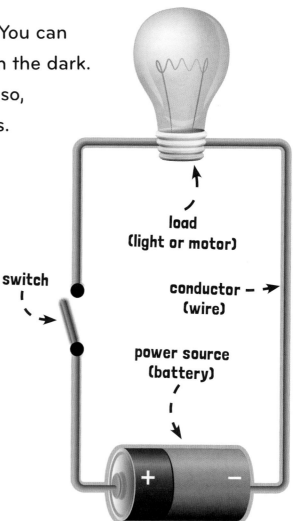

load
(light or motor)

switch

conductor — →
(wire)

power source
(battery)

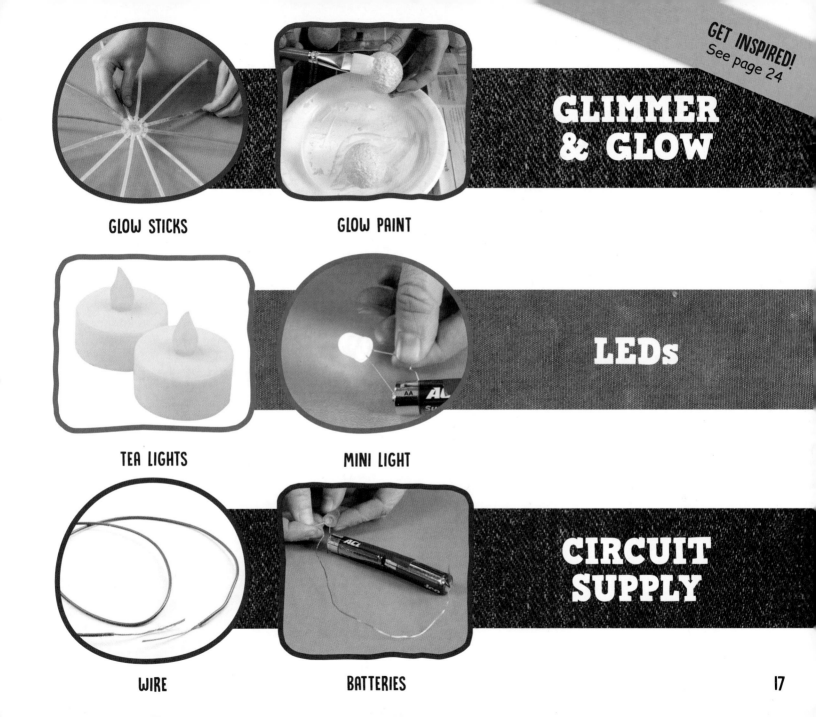

GET INSPIRED!
See page 24

GLIMMER & GLOW

GLOW STICKS

GLOW PAINT

LEDs

TEA LIGHTS

MINI LIGHT

CIRCUIT SUPPLY

WIRE

BATTERIES

CONNECT YOUR LIGHT

Will your light be **permanent**? Or will you take it apart when you are finished? Knowing this will help you decide what materials to use.

TOTALLY TEMPORARY

| WOODEN SKEWERS | PINS | HOOK-AND-LOOP TAPE | RUBBER BANDS |

COLLABORATE!
See page 28

IMAGINE

WHAT IF YOU WERE TRAPPED ON A ROCKY CLIFF? COULD YOU MAKE YOUR LIGHT A PLANE SO IT COULD GLIDE AWAY TO FIND RESCUERS?

A LITTLE STICKY

SUPER STICKY

ELECTRICAL TAPE   GLUE STICK   HOT GLUE   GLUE DOTS

DECORATE YOUR LIGHT

Decorating is the final step in making your light. It's where you add **details** to your creation. How do these decorations help your light do its job?

SPLASH OF COLOR

PAINT

PAPER

STICKERS

IMAGINE

WHAT IF YOU WANTED YOUR LIGHT TO SHINE GREEN? WHAT MATERIALS COULD YOU USE TO CAST THIS COLOR?

GET INSPIRED!
See page 24

SOLID STYLE

SPARKLE & SHINE

DUCT TAPE

JUICE BOTTLE CAP

GLOW GLITTER GLUE

SPARKLY TAPE

CELLOPHANE

21

HELPFUL HACKS

As you work, you might discover ways to make challenging tasks easier. Try these simple tricks and **techniques** as you build your light!

Use a screw **mechanism** to open and close your circuit.

Surround your light with reflective materials. This will help your **gadget** give off more light.

Use foam to wedge objects firmly in place.

PROBLEM-SOLVE!
See page 26

Use clear, sturdy materials for an **invisible** structure.

Make sure you have a way to easily operate your circuit's switch.

Use a spinning motor to give your light motion.

⚠ STUCK?

MAKERS AROUND THE WORLD SHARE THEIR PROJECTS ON THE INTERNET AND IN BOOKS. IF YOU HAVE A MAKERSPACE PROBLEM, THERE'S A GOOD CHANCE SOMEONE ELSE HAS ALREADY FOUND A SOLUTION. SEARCH THE INTERNET OR LIBRARY FOR HELPFUL ADVICE AS YOU MAKE YOUR PROJECTS!

GET INSPIRED

Get inspiration from the real world before you start building your light!

In any home you'll find **gadgets** for lighting up rooms, closets, stairways, and more. Look at the **designs** of the lights around your home. What features make them perfect for a certain task or area?

Humans lit up the dark long before electricity. Ancient civilizations burned animal fats in lamps made from rocks, shells, and horns. In the West Indies islands, people collected fireflies! These flying insects naturally glow in the dark.

LOOK AT EMERGENCY GEAR

Lights are often part of **emergency** gear. Flashlights, candles, and glow sticks are helpful when power is out. Life vests are often fitted with lights so wearers can be spotted in the dark.

PROBLEM-SOLVE

No makerspace project goes exactly as planned. But with a little creativity, you can find a **solution** to any problem.

FIGURE OUT THE PROBLEM

Maybe your glow-stick hat isn't staying on your head. Why do you think this is happening? Thinking about what may be causing the problem can lead you to a solution!

SOLUTION:
ADD A PART TO YOUR HAT THAT BETTER HUGS YOUR HEAD.

SOLUTION:
ADD A CHIN STRAP THAT YOU CAN TIGHTEN FOR A SNUG FIT.

BRAINSTORM AND TEST

Try coming up with three possible **solutions** to any problem.
Maybe your flashlight's LED isn't lighting up.
You could:

1. Try again with new wires, new **batteries**, or both.

2. Experiment with an electronics kit, such as Squishy Circuits or littleBits.

3. Decorate or adapt an already-working light to serve your survival needs.

ADAPT

Still stuck? Try a different material or change the **technique** slightly.

COLLABORATE

Collaboration means working together with others. There are tons of ways to collaborate to create a light!

ASK A FELLOW MAKER - - - -

Don't be shy about asking a friend or classmate for help on your project. Other makers can help you think through the different steps to building a light. These helpers can also lend a hand during construction!

ASK AN ADULT HELPER

This could be a parent, teacher, grandparent, or any trusted adult. Tell this person about your light's most important function or feature. Your grown-up helper might think of materials or **techniques** you never would have thought of!

ASK AN EXPERT

An electrician could teach you the basics of creating circuits. A lighting **designer** could explain how light creates exciting effects in plays and movies.

29

THE WORLD IS A MAKERSPACE!

Your light may look finished, but don't close your makerspace toolbox yet. Think about what would make your **gadget** better. What would you do differently if you built it again? What would happen if you used different **techniques** or materials?

IMAGINATION

INSPIRATION

COLLABORATION

PROBLEM-SOLVING

DON'T STOP AT LIGHTS

You can use your makerspace toolbox beyond the makerspace! You might use it to accomplish everyday tasks, such as folding clothes or working on a group project. But makers use the same toolbox to do big things. One day, these tools could help build homes or make cities cleaner. Turn your world into a makerspace! What problems could you solve?

GLOSSARY

battery – a small container filled with chemicals that makes electrical power.

beacon – a signal used for guidance.

collaborate – to work with others.

dangerous – able or likely to cause harm or injury.

design – to plan how something will appear or work. A design is a sketch or outline of something that will be made. A designer is someone who plans how something will appear or work.

detail – a small part of something.

emergency – a sudden, unexpected, dangerous situation that requires immediate attention.

flexible – easy to move or bend.

gadget – a small tool that does a particular job.

invisible – unable to be seen.

mechanism – a system of parts working together.

permanent – meant to last for a very long time.

refract – to cause a ray, such as light, to bend when it passes at an angle from one medium into another, such as from air into water.

solution – an answer to, or a way to solve, a problem.

technique – a method or style in which something is done.